Who Makes a FOREST?

SALLY NICHOLLS & CAROLINA RABEI

ANDERSEN PRESS

Who makes a forest?
Is it a wizard or a giant?
A business corporation?
An emperor and all
their armies?

No.
First, you have bare,
stony ground.
No earth.
Nothing that holds water.
Nowhere to put down roots.

What comes first?
Not an English rose
or a mighty oak,
but tiny,
clinging plants.

Little smears of green on the stone.
Lichen. Algae. Moss.
What comes next?

Insects. Beetles. Ants.

Busy, crawling things, who eat the moss
and fertilise the ground.

They die, and the moss dies.
And tiny microscopic
creatures come, and break
their bodies into soil.

So now there is soil, and in the soil,

and in the plants, there is water.

And little seeds blow in on the wind,

and now there are ferns, and grass,
and wild flowers in the stony places.

Bees come, and butterflies.

And the flowers may be small, but their roots bury
down into cracks in the rock

and they wear the rocks into stones, and the stones
into pebbles, and the pebbles into earth.

There's shade now. Thistles grow, and brambles,
spiky, hardy plants.

Birds stay, and eat the blackberries,
and the worms, and the beetles.

Mice come, and rats, and
voles, and hedgehogs.

They die, and the plants die, and
their bodies sink into the leaf
mould and thicken the soil.

Shrubs grow.
Sycamore keys whirl in,
and saplings sprout in the cracks
in the rocks, and the cracks widen, and the
leaf mould settles, and now, if you look,
there's more earth there
than stone.

Years pass.
Decades. Centuries.
And what was once a bare
and barren land
is now a forest.

Deer graze in the shade of the trees.
Flowers grow by the side
of the streams.

More things live and grow here than
you could count in a lifetime.

And who made the forest?
A wizard, a giant,
an emperor?

No.
It was the seeds
and the bees and the
roots of the trees.
It was a thousand,
thousand tiny things.

And together they changed the face of the earth.

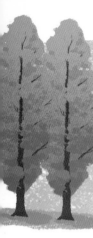

FORESTS AROUND THE WORLD

Forests are one of the most incredible and varied habitats on earth. They contain trees of all shapes and sizes, some bearing fruit or nuts, some with needles or leaves, and some that change colour with the seasons. Forests are home to animals, fish, insects, fungi and people, too! Amazingly, eight out of ten land-based species live in forests around the world.

Forests cover nearly one third of the world's land-surface – more than 15.3 million square miles – and we share the earth with a staggering **three trillion trees** which help to keep our air clean and our planet healthy.

Our perfect partners on earth, trees **absorb the carbon dioxide** that we breathe out, then they **release the oxygen** we breathe in. Trees also **absorb many of the polluting gases** we create by industry, making them essential for the survival of our planet.

Weird and wonderful forests can be found all over the world, such as the **arid thorn forests of India**, filled with succulents and euphorbia, and the **bamboo forests of China** that are home to the giant panda. There are many kinds of forest, each with their own unique mix of plants and animals, but in general there are three main types of forest which can be categorised by their distance from the equator: warm and wet **tropical** forests, mild **temperate** forests and snowy **boreal** forests.

BOREAL

TEMPERATE

Tropic of Cancer

Equator

TROPICAL

Tropic of Capricorn

TEMPERATE

The **largest** forest in the world is the **Amazon Rainforest**, which stretches across **nine countries** in South America over 2.1 million square miles, and has existed on earth for **over 55 million years**.

The **oldest** forest in the world is thought to be the **Daintree Rainforest** in Australia. At a whopping **100 – 180 million years old**, it is old enough to have been a home to **dinosaurs**.

TROPICAL FORESTS

LOCATION: Between the Tropic of Cancer in the north and the Tropic of Capricorn in the south.

AVERAGE ANNUAL RAINFALL: 200 to 1,000cm

TEMPERATURE: 20°C to 34°C with no clear seasons.

Located in areas closest to the equator, **tropical rainforests** are warm, wet, and rich with plant and animal life. Over half of the world's plant and animal species can be found in tropical forests. Some, like the Monteverde in Costa Rica, are called 'cloud forests', because they are often covered in low-lying foggy clouds.

Hummingbird

Capuchin monkey

Harpy eagle

Kapok tree

Macaw parrots

The **emergent layer**, composed of trees that tower over the canopy, is unique to tropical forests. It's bright and windy and is home to small monkeys, insects and birds.

Sloth

Fruit and nuts grow in the **canopy** in abundance, perfect for many of the rainforest's inhabitants, including sloths and fruit bats.

Strangler vines

The **understorey** is warm and damp, and full of shade-loving plants. Larger predators can be found here, such as the jaguar.

Orangutan

On the **forest floor** it is dark, hot and damp. Dead leaves from the layers above rot and decay, providing the perfect home for insects, fungi and the animals that eat them.

Jaguar

Anteater

The soil of the tropical rainforest is waterlogged and not very nutritious, so many trees have buttress roots, which allow them to absorb as much nutrition as possible and also prevent them from falling.

Giant centipedes that hunt on the forest floor can grow up to 12 inches in length!

TEMPERATE FORESTS

LOCATION: USA, Canada, Europe, China, Japan, New Zealand, Chile, Australia, Tasmania.
AVERAGE ANNUAL RAINFALL: 75 to 150cm
TEMPERATURE: -30°C to 30°C with four distinct seasons.

The forest in our story is a **temperate forest**. These forests grow further away from the equator than rainforests, they are less warm and have four distinct seasons. The trees that grow in temperate forests are mostly deciduous, meaning that they shed their leaves in autumn and regrow them in spring, which makes for glorious displays of oranges and reds in autumn, and rich greens in spring and summer. Many of the animals here have adapted to the cold winters and warm summers.

Oak trees can live for hundreds of years, and their acorns are food for many of the creatures that live here.

Moderate temperatures and rainfall provide the perfect conditions for leaf decay to create fertile soil.

Snowy owl

The leaves of **deciduous** trees change colour in the autumn because the tree stops producing chlorophyll, which is what gives them their green colour.

Oak tree

Fungi don't just live on the forest floor, some live on the trees. Wood infected by the **Beefsteak fungus** is prized by furniture-makers for its particular brown colour.

Birch tree

Hazel tree

Deciduous trees lose their leaves in the autumn to prevent water loss through their leaves during winter.

Hazel catkins

Deer don't hibernate, but they eat the bark and shoots of trees, and can dig under snow to reach plants that keep their leaves in winter.

Fox

Rabbit

Moles dig deeper when the ground freezes over and don't return to the surface as often.

Hedgehogs hibernate in the colder months.

Squirrels store nuts and seeds in shallow pits in the summer, ready for wintertime.

BOREAL FORESTS

LOCATION: Canada, Europe, Asia, USA, Northern Hemisphere only.
AVERAGE ANNUAL RAINFALL: 30 to 90cm
TEMPERATURE: -40°C to 20°C with two seasons, a long winter and a short summer.

Even further away from the equator are **boreal forests**, also known as **taiga**. Colder and drier than temperate forests, the taiga is mostly made up of evergreen coniferous trees that have water-retaining needles instead of leaves, and cones instead of flowers. Summers are short and winter temperatures can get very cold, so only the hardiest and most adaptable of animals and insects live here.

Snow geese stay in the taiga all year round, and do not migrate south.

The **Luna moth** only lives for seven days once it has left its cocoon. Their adult lives are so short-lived, they do not have mouths and never eat.

Fir tree

Pine tree

Coniferous needles

Cone

Great grey owl

Beavers create dead wood by felling trees for food and to build their dams. Dead wood is an essential habitat for many insects and fungi that live in the taiga.

Forest fires are common, and essential to the life-cycle of some of the creatures that live here. **Black fire beetles** can sense the heat of forest fires to help them search for freshly burned trees, where they lay their eggs.

Bears

Wolf

Lichen, mosses, mushrooms and conifer trees thrive on thin soil that lacks nutrients.

Spruce tree

Elk

Snowshoe hare

Carpenter ants store food underground throughout the year to sustain them during cold winters.

WHAT ARE WE DOING TO OUR FORESTS?

Forests don't just provide a habitat for animals and plants, over 300 million people call forests their home. Since the dawn of man, forests have provided us with shelter, food and raw materials for buildings, art and medicine. They are often referred to as 'the lungs of the earth', helping to absorb harmful carbon dioxide in our atmosphere. Forests are vital to life on earth, but they are disappearing fast, even within our lifetime.

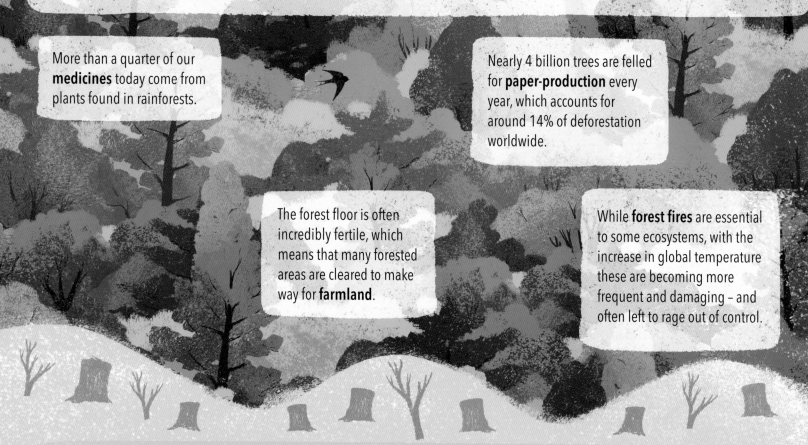

More than a quarter of our **medicines** today come from plants found in rainforests.

Nearly 4 billion trees are felled for **paper-production** every year, which accounts for around 14% of deforestation worldwide.

The forest floor is often incredibly fertile, which means that many forested areas are cleared to make way for **farmland**.

While **forest fires** are essential to some ecosystems, with the increase in global temperature these are becoming more frequent and damaging – and often left to rage out of control.

Deforestation is the clearing of forests, often in order to put the land or materials to another use. Nearly half of all deforestation is because of farming and livestock production, but there are many other reasons: timber production, mining and urbanisation are just a few. These human needs, along with the rise in forest fires due to an increase in global temperatures, have contributed to the loss of around 40% of the world's forests, and it is estimated that an area of forest the size of the UK is destroyed every year.

Planting new forests is often offered as one solution to the problem of deforestation, but many naturally occurring forests have been standing for thousands, or sometimes millions of years and have developed complex ecosystems that cannot be replicated in a short time by replanting. The best solution to the effects of deforestation is prevention.

WHAT CAN WE DO?

We can all make a difference by making little changes to our everyday lives, here are a few you can try today!

- **Try to use wood products that come from sustainable sources.**
- **Reuse and recycle when possible.**
- **Avoid buying products that contain unsustainable palm oil.**
- **Try to eat less meat to reduce the land used for grazing.**
- **Buy from companies that are environmentally friendly.**